# MAN V. LIVER

## NEIL HINSON
## PAUL FRIEDRICH

D1710475

# MAN V. LIVER

Dedicated to my liver.
*Keep up the good work, Champ!*

**Introductory Note**

Everyone has that friend that keeps them out too late. Tries to turn a Tuesday happy hour into a Friday free-for-all. This friend will crack open your can of secrets with the simple formula of equal parts shots and beers. Repeat.

You laugh with this person into the night, maybe even share a slurry cab ride. But you heal from your hangover alone under the bright fluorescent of your next workday.

I am that friend. This is my battle.

**Man v. Liver**

ANYTHING IS ACCEPTABLE, AS LONG AS IT'S HOT AND BRIGHT AND A FEW GIRLS ARE AROUND.

# Secrets of Chicago

It's windy here sometimes, and cats fly through the air with their claws outstretched, hoping to get gusted into a tree or a lady's stockings. Have you ever seen that happen? They're like little furry superheroes!
I can't find any ice cream in Chicago yet, though. I sure hope they have some, cause ice cream's tasty and makes having a cat stuck to your slacks a lot less irritating. And if so, what flavors? Do Chicagoans know about chocolate and rocky road, or are those just beloved by down-south racists and race-mixers? Such an exciting city!

Speaking of race mixers, I want to go to parties with different races. I mean black and white and brown folks–not car races or foot races. I hear that, because of the jazz music that black people play here while they tap their feet, that blonde women are often seduced into shaking their thing. So that sounds fun. Shake those pusses right off their stockings.

In other big news, I met a blonde girl Saturday night with a very cute, funny nose. I would say that I'll cherish that memory forever, but like a poor Xerox, I remember it in blurry triplicate.

In even other news, I would like to be rich. I could hire jazz musicians to come to my house to entice all the blonde women with cute noses in town to stop by, shake it and drink.

SLEPT IN MY CLOTHES
LAST NIGHT. WHICH
MEANS I WAS THE
BEST-DRESSED AT
BREAKFAST.

SCREW IT.
IT'S NOON
SOMEWHERE.

HINSON &
Friedrich

# IF A TREE MAKES A DOUBLE ALBUM IN THE WOODS DOES ANYONE LISTEN TO IT?

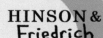

HINSON &
Friedrich

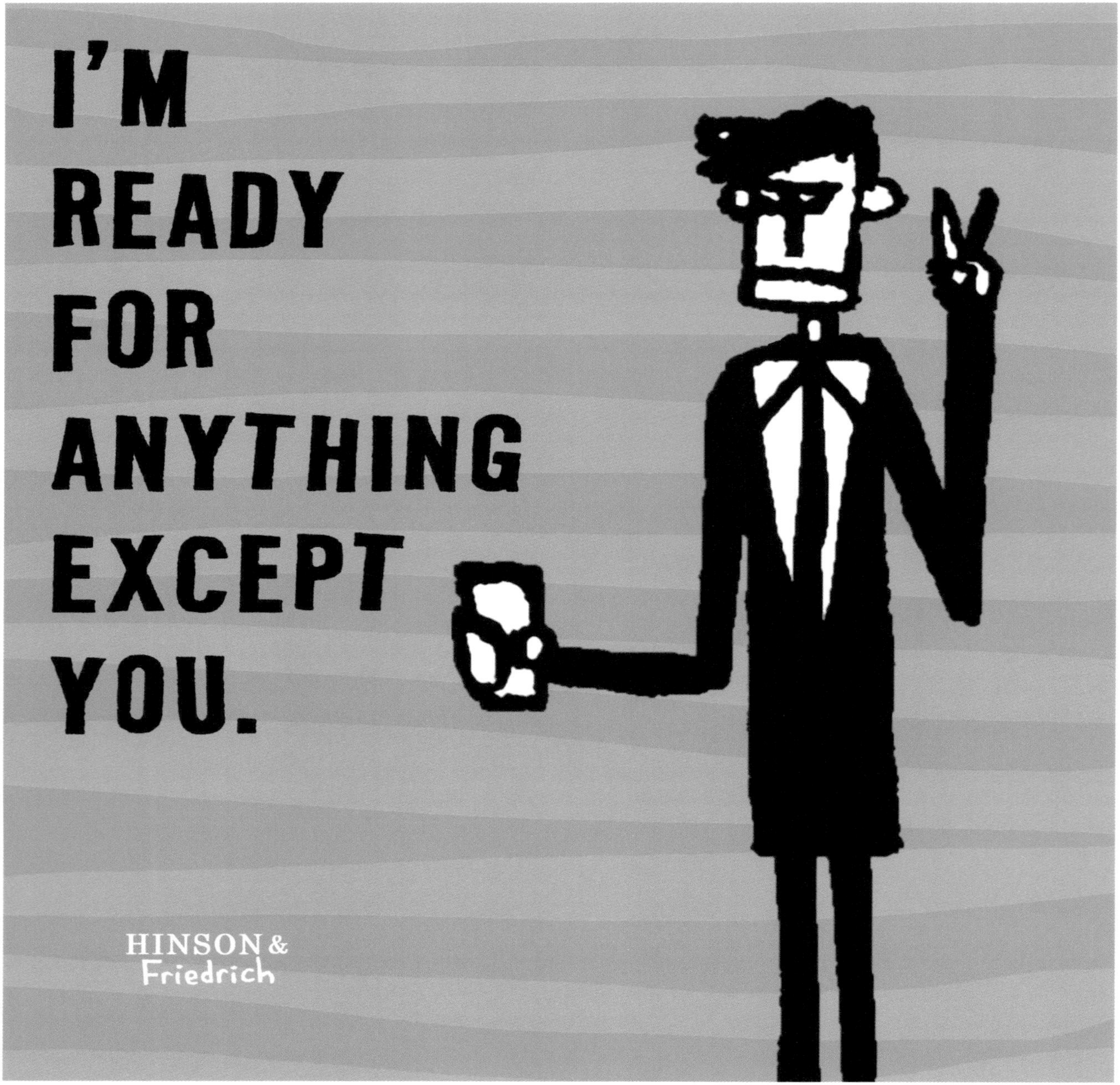
I'M READY FOR ANYTHING EXCEPT YOU.
HINSON & Friedrich

# AM I BLURRING MY WORDS?

HINSON & Friedrich

IF YOU SEE ME GETTING SMALLER THAT MEANS YOU'RE LEAVING.

HINSON & Friedrich

I LOVE WOMEN ~~WHO~~
~~TALK ABOUT~~
~~CHOCOLATE~~
~~CATS~~
~~MIXED DRINKS~~
~~AND SHOES.~~

HINSON &
Friedrich

HOW'S YOUR FRIEND
FROM PORTLAND?
THE WAGONEER.

HINSON &
Friedrich

# I'M BLANKING ON YOUR NAME BUT I REMEMBER YOUR DRINK. AND THAT'S WHAT'S IMPORTANT. TO ME.

HINSON &
Friedrich

SIMPLY AWESOME.

HINSON &
Friedrich

# I TEND TO REACT TO MY OWN WEAKNESS WITH STRENGTH.

I CHARTERED
THE WATERS
YOU'RE DROWNING IN.

HINSON &
Friedrich

# I GOT ANTS IN MY PANTS. I SENSE YOU HAVE CRABS.

HINSON &
Friedrich

# OFFER ME A COSMO, HEAR MY LIVER GIGGLE.

HINSON & Friedrich

# IF YOU WERE ANY DUMBER I'D HAVE TO WATER YOU.

KNOW WHAT
MAKES A
GREAT
DRINKING GAME?

DRINKING.

HINSON &
Friedrich

# MY EYES WERE BIGGER THAN MY LIVER.

HINSON &
Friedrich

# MY DOCTOR ASKED ME IF I WANTED A FLU SHOT. HE WAS HALF RIGHT.

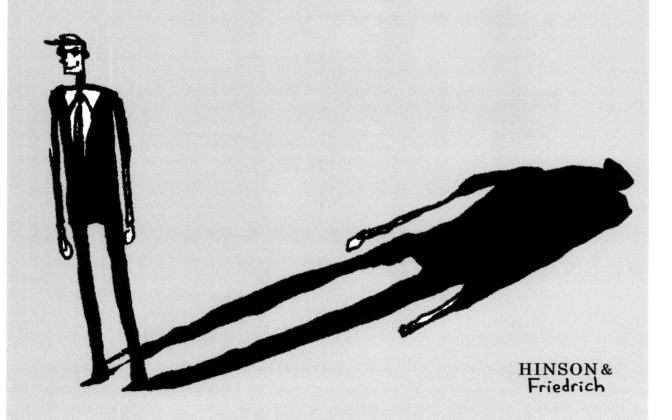

I DON'T NEED A GLASS. IT ALREADY IS IN A GLASS. IT'S CALLED A BOTTLE.

HINSON & Friedrich

# FOUR SCORES AND 7 SCOTCHES AGO...

HINSON &
Friedrich

# NICE PHONE.
# DOUCHEBAG.

HINSON &
Friedrich

# SOBRIETY IS MY HALLOWEEN COSTUME.

# THIS IS WORTH THE HANGOVER

HINSON &
Friedrich

# In Praise of Half Empty

Optimistic folks like to describe themselves as seeing a glass 'half full.' That's fine for PTA meetings, urban planners and ants pushing rubber tree plants.

But people who know the elegant power of alcohol know it's better to be 'half empty.'

Because a half-empty glass means your blood is bubbling with manna, and your brain is ascending the Elevator of Happiness ('next floor: cheerleaders, laughter, making out…'). You're halfway to wrestling alligators for the imperiled supermodel. And halfway willing to dance.

Look at it this way, if you're on the trail to Heaven, wouldn't you rather be halfway there than halfway away from where you started?

So here's to half empty, and the half-light of inebriation.

TWITTER.
TEXTING.
POSTING.
IS ANYONE
HERE
ACTUALLY
HERE?

HINSON &
Friedrich

THE MARKET HAS
BEER ON SALE.

SEE, YOU CAN
PUT A PRICE
ON HAPPINESS.

HINSON &
Friedrich

I AM HERE
TO WHERE
THERE
IS BEER.

HINSON &
Friedrich

HANG ON,
MY DRINK'S
CALLING ME.

HINSON &
Friedrich

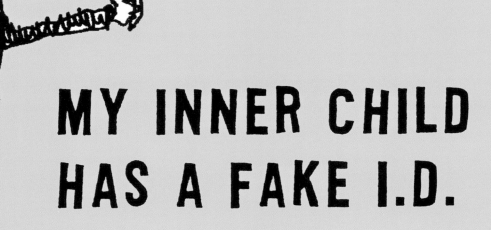

MY INNER CHILD
HAS A FAKE I.D.

HINSON &
Friedrich

HINSON &
Friedrich

# THIS IS WHY I DON'T KEEP A JOURNAL.

I DON'T BELIEVE IN LABELS.

UNLESS THEY'RE FROM PARIS.

HINSON & Friedrich

# I THINK.
# THEREFORE
# I DRINK.

HINSON &
Friedrich

LIVE
FREE
AND
DRINK UP

HINSON &
Friedrich

SOME PEOPLE
LIVE IT.
I DRINK IT.

HINSON &
Friedrich

A MONKEY
COULD DO
MY JOB.
HE JUST
COULDN'T
GET DENTAL
INSURANCE.

# THAT WAS A WASTE OF MY NECK MUSCLES.

HINSON &
Friedrich

## Insectus Imbibus

OK, so nobody likes to share their gin, especially on a summer day, and especially not with a bug. But hey, maybe this bee had been working hard and mistook my Sapphire for a glittery wading pool. You know, a post honey-hunt wetdown. Or maybe bees are just really dumb.

Anyway, one minute I'm prying a phone number from our waitress, the next, boom – or rather, splash – I've got a little stranger floating near my lime. Silence fell over the table.

The first comment to crack the shock: 'Huh. Bees float.'

So I dip my little stirrer stick into my drink and flip the carcass onto the table. Sad, I thought, the fella's first taste of the spirit is his last. Talk resumed. Phone numbers were re-pursued. The sun dipped in the sky.

Then it happened. The creature stirred and stood up. Or tried to, tumbling backwards, its wings making zombie flips. The spiny feet started pushing forward in a dazed zigzag toward the table's edge.

'You can do it!' I yelled, as the moment overtook me ('Do what?' I then thought.)

The bee seemed to take in one last steadying breath, then heaved itself off the table. It dropped like a buzzing pebble, disappearing from view. Then, like a Phoenix or a little fuzzy Wright Brother, liftoff. It left us in a sagging arc, up and down, left to right.

'Not exactly a beeline,' someone said.

IF YOU DON'T WANT ME TO STARE AT YOUR CHEST, DON'T HOLD YOUR MARTINI NEAR IT.

HINSON & Friedrich

I FEED OFF
PEER PRESSURE.

HINSON &
Friedrich

EXPIRED
PASSPORT.
BUT I CAN
STILL GO
ON A BENDER.

HINSON &
Friedrich

# WAS THAT MY OUTLOUD VOICE?

# PIECE, BABY

HINSON &
Friedrich

I'M NOT LANDING PLANES HERE.

HINSON & Friedrich

HANGOVERS CAN FEEL LIKE PUNISHMENT. BUT SOBRIETY IS A LIFE SENTENCE.

HINSON & Friedrich

IT'S NOT RAINING IN HERE, WHY DOES YOUR DRINK HAVE AN UMBRELLA?

HINSON &
Friedrich

I REMEMBER LESS
BUT I REGRET LESS TOO.

HINSON &
Friedrich

# "SHOO"

I SHAVED
FOR THIS?

HINSON&
Friedrich

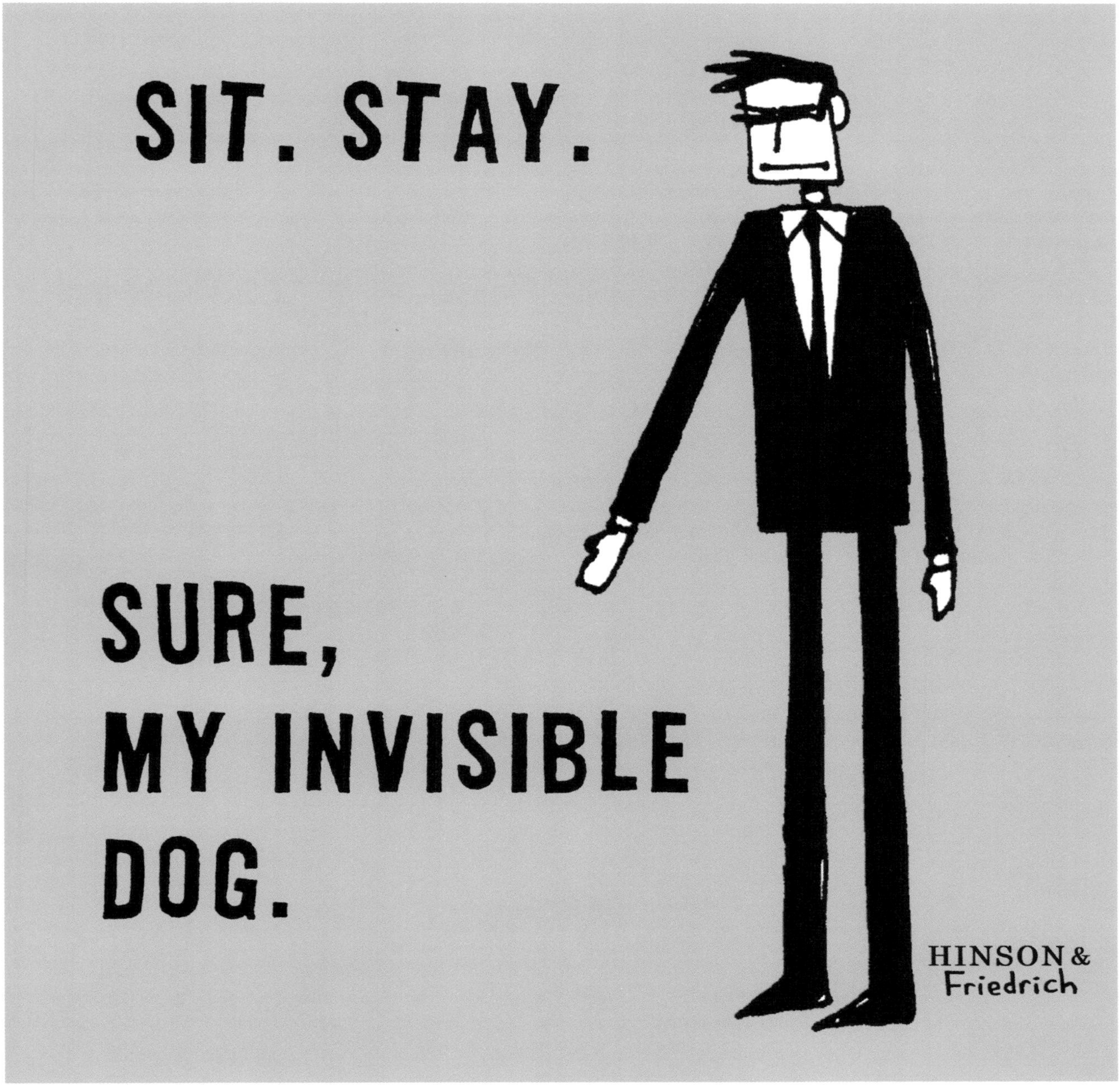
SIT. STAY.
SURE, MY INVISIBLE DOG.
HINSON & Friedrich

# IF MEN ARE FROM MARS. AND WOMEN FROM VENUS, THEN EARTH IS SPRING BREAK.

HINSON &
Friedrich

# Getting the Perfect Martini

These days, martinis can be a lot of things. Chocolate-cake flavored, apple flavored, apricot-mango flavored, ham-flavored (that one's rare, but still). Basically anything in a martini glass qualifies now. But purists know there's only one real martini, and here's how it should be prepared:

Go to a bar. A crowded one.

Stand near someone who's just ordered a drink.

Tell him or her that someone across the room likes the way they look. Point at someone attractive.

Talk about this, how exciting, how sexy, the evening is about to get. Let the bartender see your conversation.

Tell him or her (OK, him. A girl's not going to fall for this.) it's time to stone-up and go speak with her.

As he leaves, order a martini. Shaken, dry, with gin. Or however the hell you like it. Tell the bartender it's on your friend's tab.

Because the perfect martini is a free martini.

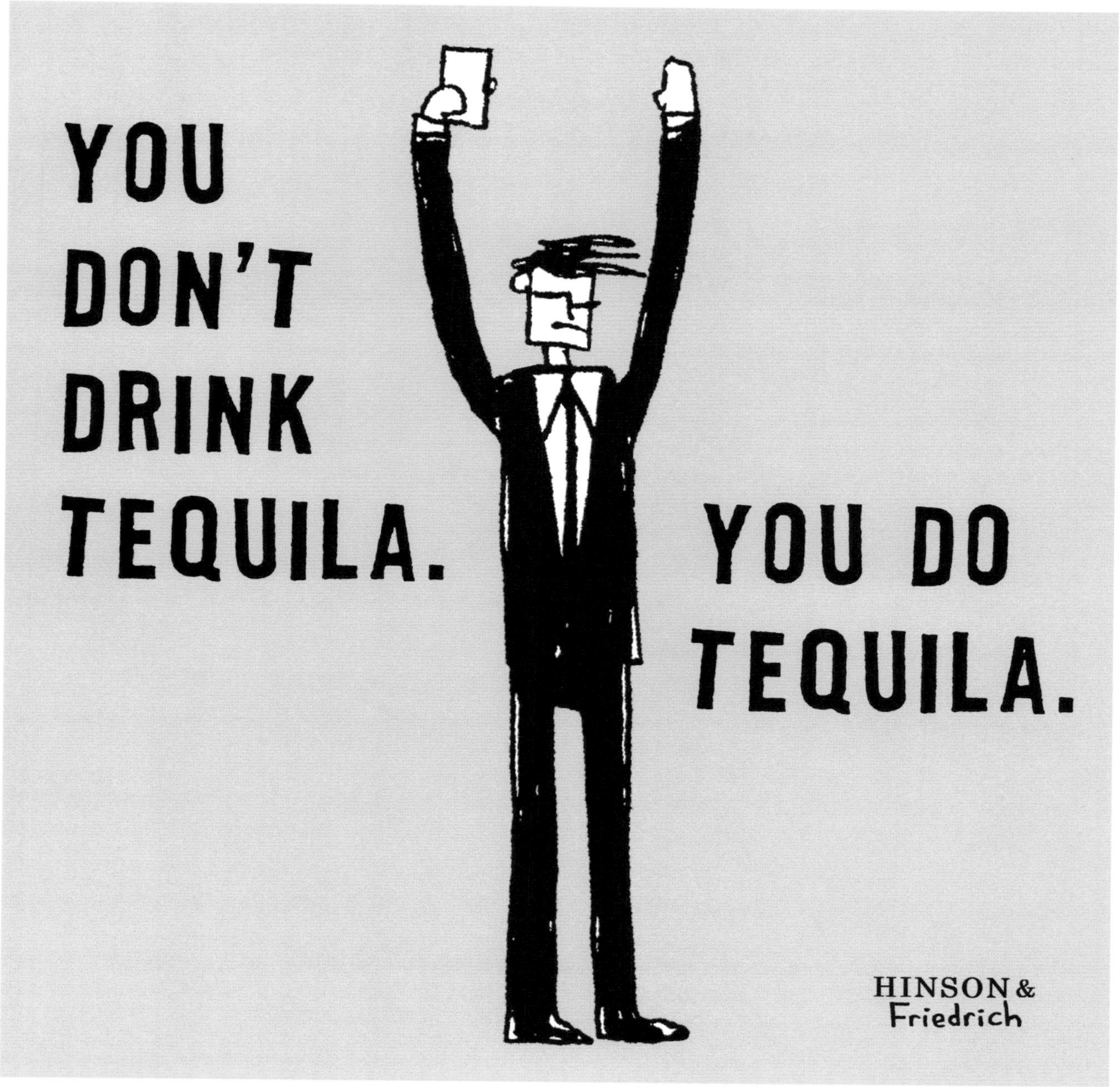
YOU DON'T DRINK TEQUILA.
YOU DO TEQUILA.
HINSON & Friedrich

# THINKING HARD WITHOUT HARDLY THINKING

HINSON &
Friedrich

# PEACE ON EARTH AND A THREESOME. NOT NECESSARILY IN THAT ORDER.

THAT GIRL IS
SUPER TIKI.

HINSON &
Friedrich

I EAT GUYS LIKE
YOU FOR BREAKFAST.
OR TOAST.

HINSON &
Friedrich

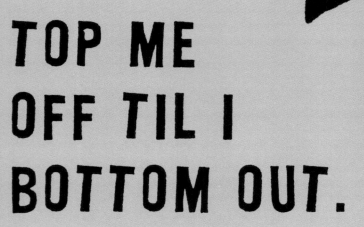

AS SEEN ON TV

HINSON &
Friedrich

# I LIKE MY SCRAMBLED EGGS SCRAMBLED.

Made in the USA
Charleston, SC
07 September 2011